Simple Living

....

THE PATH
TO JOY AND FREEDOM

José Hobday

CONTINUUM • NEW YORK

2002

The Continuum Publishing Company
370 Lexington Avenue
New York, NY 10017

Copyright © 1998 by José Hobday

Printed in the United States of America

Library of Congress Cataloging-in-Publication Data

Hobday, José
    Simple living : the path to joy and freedom / José Hobday.
    p.   cm.
    ISBN 0-8264-0846-X (pbk.)
    1. Simplicity—Religious aspects—Christianity. 2. Christian
life—Catholic authors   I. Title.
  BV4647.S48H63   1998
  248.8—dc 21   98-30172
                                                       CIP

Contents

Freedoms of Simplicity

Simplicity is one of those great words that can't be defined easily. But it can be described and it can be distinguished from things that just look a little like it. If we persevere, we can recognize simplicity when we experience it in others and, more importantly, when we practice it.

Simple living is not about elegant frugality. It is not really about deprivation of whatever is useful and helpful for our life. It is not about harsh rules and stringent regulations. To live simply, one has to consider all of these and they may be included to some degree, but simple living is about freedom. It's about a freedom to choose space rather than clutter, to choose open and generous living rather than a secure and sheltered way.

Freedom is about choices: Freedom to choose less rather than more. It's about choosing time for people and ideas and self-growth rather than for maintenance and guarding and possessing and cleaning. Simple living is about moving through life rather lightly, delighting in the plain and the subtle. It is about poetry and dance, song and art, music and grace. It is about optimism and humor, gratitude and appreciation. It is about embracing life with wide-open arms. It's about living and giving with no strings attached.

Simple living has fewer knots and more bows than scattered and cluttered living. More standing on tiptoe, more quiet waiting. More openness to the next moment. Or the next day. Or the next year. The options are more obvious if one is living simply. So are the choices.

Simple living is as close as the land on which we stand. It is as far-reaching as the universe that makes us gasp. Simple living is a relaxed grasp on money, things, and even friends. Simplicity cherishes ideas and relationships. They are treasured more because simplicity doesn't cling nor try to possess things or people or relationships. Simplicity frees us within, but it frees others, too. People don't have to compliment our clothing or admire our collections. They aren't distracted from what's real. Simple living is a statement of presence. The real me. This simplicity makes us welcome among the wealthy and the poor alike. The poor are not offended by our dress and the rich are not threatened. This applies to clothing, housing, and transportation. To live simply we have to live in such a way that simple people feel welcome in our home. When they come to visit, they don't have to worry that they might soil good furniture or break expensive glassware or leave fingerprints on something precious.

The path to simple living may be narrow and winding or it can be wide and quite straight. Both flowers and stickers will grow along the way. Simple living gives a lilt to the spirit and a lightness to the step, with surprises aplenty. Even the thistles cross our road buoyantly. They are the tumbling tumbleweeds in our path.

Simple living is not easy. This is difficult to understand at first. It is not difficult to live a scattered, fragmented, harried, disconnected life. It is difficult to stay focused, to live out of a center that allows for calm choices and considered decisions.

Easy and simple are not interchangeable terms, at least not for the first twenty years! Attending to simple living yields unsuspected abundance, joy and freedom. Having things that are meaningful to us contributes to simple living. We need to ponder this. We have to know what matters in our life. We have to meditate on our own priorities. Some people really enjoy souvenirs, others like certain colors. Some just love clothing. Others love jewelry.

So part of simplicity is knowing what you really like and what helps you. The reason I can travel around the world with two basic dresses is because I love simplicity. I really love those two dresses. They're flowered dresses and I consider that I am wearing my own gardens! I have pants and a shirt and a sweater for traveling. I wear them with the freedom that I don't care if a flight attendant spills something on me or if the child next to me throws up on me. I have no concern about a ruined wardrobe when I'm traveling.

In speaking of simplicity, I am speaking of a way of life that flows from an inner stance. It is an attitude. It requires discernment of emphasis. It requires that we decide what we want to accentuate in life. That means it will take time to attend to this and evaluate it. It will require that we think about where we are going. And just as important, why.

We will pause along the way, not just to evaluate simplicity but to appreciate it. We will want to taste simplicity, smack our lips over it and rejoice in our life situation. We might even consider that it is recreation.

I think it is the promise of freedom that really attracts us to simplicity, that it is the desire to expand and explore. For me, it has always been natural. I learned it from my parents. We were taught that the value of things is not in things. Every thing is a helper, a friend. Not only the four-leggeds and the swimmies, the creepies and the crawlies and the wingeds, but things like rocks and stars and the winds. All of these things are helpers. Once you understand that everything is on your side, and that it has a life of its own, that it is part of your conscious life, you are freer and more confident. We always withstood the desire to own our mother, the earth. We Native Americans resisted people trying to tell us that we could cut her up and sell her. We understood the earth as a form in itself, a presence to be protected, loved, and respected.

We used to say you could tell if a person was an authentic native by whether or not she had a red heart. A red heart had to do with whether the heart had blood from being massaged by good works, especially sharing. Native people have never understood the value of money for its own sake . . . have never understood the value of work just to get ahead. Work was to provide what was needed to beautify the world. Work was to decorate. Native Americans have always felt that the key to forceful living is celebration. Celebrate everything. Your pot, your plate, your food, tribal heritage, rivers, trees—everything is to be celebrated, not owned and possessed. Division was at the heart of real trouble and a cause for lack of peace. The native tradition is always to seek harmony. If you have many needs and desires, harmony is not possible. For harmony you need movement, the rhythm to go with life. Part of the rhythm of life is supplied by the singing of people as well as by the singing of birds and the music of the winds. Some harmony is supplied by learning to live with the living and the dead.

We cannot hang on to Spring, no matter how much we like it. Spring turns into Summer; you cannot hold it back. All creation has movement. It is cyclical. The secret of the simple person is to let himself or herself be carried by the harmony and rhythm of all creation. The alternative is to be stuck—to be out of step.

Simplicity keeps you walking with what is, with reality. Simple living forces you to attend to value, insisting on quality over quantity.

The Problem

Why are we so concerned with simple living? Why does it require so much effort to live simply? What is it that gets in our way? Let's examine a few of these blocks to simple living to see if they resonate with your experience.

The first serious impediment is our culture. We live in a consumption-oriented society. We are driven by the profit motive in much of our life and all of our business. We need to know that even if these are not our personal preferences or choices, they certainly influence us. This is the American lifestyle. Whether we like it or not, we are constantly being bombarded with these values of having, having still more and hoarding, then comparing how well we do that with how everyone is doing the same. We live in a materialistic society that cries for a spirit counterpart.

We are told what kind of body and face to have, we are given consumer images of our bodies and faces. We are told what skin color and texture is best, what color of hair to prefer and of course, how many pounds to weigh. We are force-fed an education in what is chic, what is hip, what is acceptable and what is not. Everywhere we turn, an image is offered. It is not the image of a healthy, giving, loving, generous, robust and full-hearted man or woman. Not that kind of image at all. Rather, we are offered an image that is slim, selfish, egocentric and vain, that does not call us to generosity. The image says to worry about yourself. Keep thinking about number one. The theme is me. More me. All me. Always me. Real happiness is subordinate to appearance, prestige and to what others will think of us.

We need to be acutely aware that advertising is the primary vehicle of this spiritually emaciated image. Our image must be dressed, fed, transported, entertained, and environmentally supported according to advertised dictates. Advertising is everywhere and in every dimension. The message is repeated: consume, buy, get, then do it some more. Gluttony is no longer a vice, it's a triumph. The two most used words in advertising are "new" and "improved." The third is "Now!" Everything must be instant and immediate. It does not allow for pacing, waiting, and setting goals.

One of the saddest remarks I have heard was before Christmas. A woman threw out her arms in a great mall and cried with pleasure, "I was born to shop!" That seems to be an illness of the American people. Our children get it early. We often maintain it throughout our life. Shop, spend, accumulate, waste. These will bury the desire for simple living.

Simplicity in a culture like ours requires companionship with people who have a different set of values. It really takes an understanding you can only get by talking through these things with your mates and friends and family. Before we talk about rearing children with these values, they have to be clear to us. We have to recognize that we are under air attack. War is being waged against generosity and simple living. Having less or doing without is cultural heresy. We will be considered practically insane if we share extravagantly, even if it is done so that others' basic needs may be met. The *giveaway* mentality of the Native is laughed at or dismissed.

One day when we were talking about life, my Dad said that everything in life is about selling. Daddy, who was a salesman, was also a purveyor of Christian thought and principle. He considered himself a gospel salesperson. He said that we really are all about selling, consciously or unconsciously. In theology, we sometimes call that witnessing. So we should make conscious choices. Do we want to sell ideas? Values? Our skills and talents? Better ways of living? Generosity and big heartedness, even greatness? Or do we want to sell only a product, an item, a machine or ourselves? These products are good and useful. But are they everything? What do we want to sell? Some people are about selling themselves, selling an image, a who or a what to an audience or to anyone they chance to meet.

Of course we sell ourselves, but the best way to sell ourselves is through what we believe in through our values and principles. When I was a little girl, my Dad said you can tell a person's faith by the way they behave. "Don't listen to what they say, look at how they live. That's where their beliefs are." So we can profess belief in gospel simplicity, we can profess belief in the leadership and sway of Christ Jesus, but we don't believe it unless we live it.

I don't mean every jot or tittle of it. We all struggle during our lives. We have some victories and some failures, but if we say we want to live the gospel it has to be clear that we know the gospel. We have to know what Jesus proclaimed. We have heard that message: "Today the blind see, the lame walk and the poor receive good news" (Luke 4:18). We see that in action because of the lives of people who minister, who care, who promote good ideas and solid values. They keep profundity and meaning alive in a world that can get vapid and superficial.

You can tell if people are living by tinsel principles. You can tell if they live only on the surface, or whether they are deep and thoughtful. We all fall into traps. We're all weak, but with simplicity, a radiance shines through. We believe that as Christians. We choose to find ways into depth. We keep adventure alive and stay creative. We keep ourselves on the edge of our own faith by the way we live. Simplicity takes the time to really look at TV ads and billboards and magazines as they try to convince us of needs that are not needs at all. We can see right through their fraudulent message of instant gratification of more as the key to happiness. We don't need to believe that instant coffee and instant success are important to us.

We need to learn that we have to persevere. To live simply, we often have to go barefoot, just to feel. We have to stay on the path. We have to stop and take out the stickers along the way, but we must keep going—moving in what we understand is a value orientation. This orientation promotes our own meaning and the meaning of others. By keeping our life simple, we clear out valueless things and make space for things of real value. Thistles and cockleburs are good reminders. We are not called to live selfishly.

We will not be happy living selfishly in a small world. We must live in awareness and in association with the whole real world. Our universe. Our cosmos. Our environment. Our earth. Our air. Our water supply. Our country. Our neighbor. Our car. Our homes. All are part of simple living.

One can look a bit counter-cultural in our society if one chooses not to have it all. Resist compulsive buying and you raise questions and eyebrows. But the heart of it is that some things in our culture are not good for us as human beings. We have inherited patterns that interfere with the pursuit of life, liberty, and happiness. Some ways are just too individual and too small. We become spiritually isolated. The Native American way understands that we are related to everything. We are related to the sun and moon, bugs and plants and therefore we are a relative to all creation. Natives end their prayers with the refrain: "And for all our relatives." When you belong to life this profoundly, you don't substitute having for being. You open your dwelling to all and say, "Come in and share."

Sometimes we understand this on an individual level, but we are culturally blind to how this works on a community or the national level. I lived in southern Arizona with the Papago tribe. At one time they were self-sufficient. They made adobe for many areas of the Southwest. They raised cattle. They farmed. But then things changed. Great populations began to move into the area who came for retirement, for recreation and entertainment. Suddenly, water once used to raise crops and to feed farm animals and to make adobe was diverted for swimming pools and private recreation. The Papago people no longer had a sustainable way of life. This is an example of thoughtless living about resources and other people. Project development, big real estate sales, and a lifestyle that is beyond the resources of the land to supply will promote this. We're becoming aware of it in some areas as we kill off things. But killing off our water, even our oceans, and polluting our air, all have to do with our lifestyle. Simple living requires us to take a good look at our consumer mentality, our spending mentality, and our misunderstood right to squander the gifts and good of this world for a few so that many are deprived and suffer.

Simplicity: Getting What You Really Want

We don't want just the bare essentials. Nobody wants to live with the bare minimum. That suggests grayness and dullness. We so want to appreciate one glass of water that we will not wastefully throw it away if other people are injured or deprived. Material things can delight us, enhance our appetites, tease our minds and imaginations and make life comfortable and beautiful. We can express our creativity in gifts to others. When properly used, gifts enrich the soul. We've been talking about restricting, learning our needs and helps, preferences and luxuries, looking at ways to not pile up and accumulate and be really overwhelmed by things. But what am I to get out of this? What's in it for me? What can I expect from simplifying my life?

The first thing is an appreciation of real values. We learn to appreciate what we have. I've lived in California—north and south—for a dozen years, through earthquakes, fire, and floods. The thing that kept people from giving up when they lost everything—everything they cherished—was this: "We have each other." "We have our lives." "That picture album, as precious as it was, is nothing in comparison with the touch of this child's hand that I still have." Sometimes we have to lose it all to discover we have it all in the presence of our loved ones. It's not only we who come from dust and will return to dust. It's all these wonderful treasures, too. They too return to ashes and dust.

I want to tell you from years of experience that you can expect from simplicity a freedom of spirit you can hardly believe. There's a weight in having to dust and look after and count and care for and keep in place and store and insure so many things. So much is taken off our shoulders by disciplines of release and freedom. We gain not only material space but inner room for things that are new and exciting. We gain an uncluttered spot for something lovely and beautiful. We gain time. We have more room in our soul. Our soul feels clean and empty, swept out—uncluttered and unfettered.

In simplicity our spirit is freer to look at things, not with care and worry or as a custodian. Our spirit is free. We receive gifts with greater freedom. We don't ask, "Oh, where can I put this?" We don't have to worry about keeping that old picture that we have to drag out every time Aunt Suzie comes to show we still love her. Our attics and basements are empty and we can actually move through them. Or, we help all who gives us gifts to understand that we appreciate them and will enjoy them, but we also may pass them along. I'll keep some things. I'll treasure some things but always with the understanding that I will eventually give them away. We become proficient at recycling when we gain a sense of simplicity. Not only do we appreciate something while we have it, but we're always open to where it will be more appreciated, more useful, more delightful to someone who has less to delight in. And we will learn to give with no strings attached, and to help others give to us in the same way.

A Sense of Space

When we simplify we get a sense of spacious-ness. Not just physical space in our home, garage, yard, closet, and desk drawers, but a great sense of space in our mind and heart. There's a lack of preoccupation with things and more of a concern for what matters, both to ourselves and to others. We ask fresher questions, like How I can just stand around leisurely to make people happy? How can I use this time to read poetry or children's books or nonsense verse? How can I raise my level of delight in small non-purchased things? In a hurried life, waiting is terrible. But in a simple life, we might think about what we can do with the space of five or thirty minutes of waiting.

We learn that space not only gives us a sense of buoyancy and openness and fullness but a keen sense of delight. We suddenly have much more time to stand and look, to appreciate, to enjoy, perhaps even to contemplate. We're not so time-conscious, so constricted. We're not concerned if a cup of coffee goes cold. Reheat it or throw it away! We find we have more reading time. We take longer walks. We aren't forever dusting and replacing and rearranging things. Instead ideas and desires and possibilities crowd in on us, looking for expression. That's part of the freedom.

Freedom comes to both body and mind in the form of TIME. It comes in the way we manage our time. When we eat, how much we eat, the time we devote to eating and preparing food become important. I guarantee you, if you eat a little less and a little less often, you will eat with more relish both for your soul and body. Mild hunger awakens taste buds and our appreciation grows. Our heart becomes more grateful. But real hunger, ah! That leads to robust gratitude! A sense of freedom dances through life bringing a subtle joy that shows. We display our inward feeling of lighthearted effervescence. We just have less stuff to worry about, so we tend to have lots of secret smiles. Without chores to do, clothes to clean, things to move, we cut a lot of strings to daily tasks that get monotonous and wearisome, while other daily tasks, without so much pressure, become a delight. Have you ever gone to bed with all your tasks done? Me neither. Cherish the fact you have so much to get up for the next day.

Without so much pressure, we find it easier to wait for people to finish their sentences. We discover patience as we wait for another to finish that cup of coffee. We wait for the bus easier while we absorb what is around us instead of pawing at the ground like an eager racehorse. What we can't make happen becomes more evident. We quit trying to control what is beyond and outside our control.

Simplicity erodes stress. When we lay down some of our burdens, our anxiety level goes down. We itch to do this and that and those much less. We let go of collected burdens like we shed a hot coat in the summer. Remember the story of the Sun and Wind arguing about their powers? As the wind blew, the man held his coat closer. But with the Sun's warmth, he shed it in relief. We are like the person standing in the Sun of simplicity, taking off what we don't need because our life is less defensive and cumbersome and anxious. Our soul's temperature is a pleasant eighty degrees. As so many have said, "Less is more."

A Hungry Spirit

It's not strange that our culture promotes wanting so much. That's what the Spirit yearns for, too. More. We love abundance. The question is, more of what? More things? More stuff? More clutter? More junk? Of course not. The Spirit, our Spirit, yearns for more quality. Quality requires that we be more present to what we do and who we are. Quality requires we pay more attention to where we turn. It requires more love in our actions. We are required by the Spirit to have more love even in our looks, our sighs, our waiting. Our wanting more is not foreign. The Spirit is always straining and stretching us. Jesus says "Give, and it will be given to you. In good measure, pressed down, shaken together, running over" (Luke 6:38). He knows we want more.

Our Spirit wants more time for reflection and less time for dallying and finding ourselves short-circuited and bored. We do want to pause. We do want to wait, to admire, to be in communion. We want to think about things. We want to loll about and read poetry. We want to swim buoyantly. We like to look at gorgeous pictures. We like to stop and take time with a little child. We want to appreciate these pleasures of the Spirit but we seem too often to be rushed. We seem to be taken out of those wonderful pauses, those moments of enlightenment and awareness that say to us, "This is what matters, this is valuable."

We talk about quality time with children. We keep saying, because we have so little real time with them, that quality will make the difference. No. It is too controlled. Quality time is real time and sometimes it really takes an hour for a little child to get out what's on her heart. You can't sit down and say, "We now have five minutes of quality time, so deliver in quality. Get said what you need to say and I will listen in quality and we'll have this over with." That little guy doesn't know what you are talking about!

The truth is, life has a pace of its own. Many years ago, I read a definition of patience by Deitrich von Hildebrand. "Patience is the amount of time that anything takes to be what it is, to go where it is going, to do what it does." Ram Dass says this very thing in the title of his book, *Be Here Now.* This is anti-rush, anti-scurry. How I have always loved the title of that book. What does that title suggest? It says depth, first of all. It says to be. Don't flit and flutter. Stop. Pause. Be. And where do we do this? Right here, where we really are. What do we have to work with? Now. We don't have next year. Twenty minutes from now we might cross a street carelessly and end things. Here is where we are now. We slow down, pause, vacate, rush, in order to *remember* who we are and what we are about.

Perhaps those three words: be, here, now, can encircle us as we move through life so we are not leaping in fragments or separated from the stream of life. Three minutes from now we may be one block down the street. Then we will be there. There's a depth, a quality, an inner smile that goes with being really present, because the ultimate wonder is that we are present to ourselves. We are aware of ourselves. When we are present to ourselves, the content of our imagination comes to our service. We become creative. We *are* creative. We are open. Our attitude is toward life.

It's not that we don't do what we need to do nor go where we need to go. We do. But we travel with our minds and hearts open and aware. I remember as a child that I used to get very excited about things. I would have a high energy level and it was discouraging not to be able to get others enthused, too. I'd be really happy about something, (like how my horse smelled in the summer when it was frothy and sweaty and the smell was mixed with the smell of leather!) I would go on at great length about it. My brothers didn't want to listen on and on. My mother said, "Jo, that's wonderful that the smell excites you so much and gets you so enthused, but everybody doesn't feel that way." Don't let your enthusiasms die, but treat them like bright and dim lights on a car. When you're around people, maybe you should put your dims on a little more. When you're alone, turn on the brights. The brights want to search the land to see as far as they can. They have a fierce power to penetrate. The dims are a bit more subdued but they seem to be more proper and sensitive around others.

What does this have to do with simplicity? It has to do with the freedom to indulge yourself extravagantly and abundantly when you are intrigued or excited by something. Still, you learn to hold and treasure it in a special way. Simple people are often excited by the quality of things but cannot share them easily. The truth is, some people just don't care.

I had an experience of ecstasy with my mother when I was in the third grade. I never knew what ecstasy was, I knew nothing of spirituality as such, but I knew I had an experience so valuable that I couldn't talk about it with anybody. It was all I could do to hold it. It was unbearable to hold it even for three or four hours by myself, lying on my little bed in my closet-bedroom. I knew something sacred had happened. The simple truth that this was too much to tell anybody stayed with me for forty years until I understood the characteristics of ecstasy and could share this experience with others to help others understand their capacity for ecstasy and mystical experiences. But then, that's another book.

That was a simple experience for me and probably if I ever learned what one line of the gospels meant it was in relation to that. I don't know exactly what Jesus meant when he said not to throw your pearls before swine, but I knew it meant to me that sometimes, when we are alone, we will have insights and inspirations that we simply have to hold in our own hearts for a long time. We guard these gifts jealously until they will not be laughed at, dissipated, misunderstood or scorned by those we tell about them. Simplicity means having a strong center, a sense of self and recollection that we will not betray by dissipation.

I learned, on some deep level, that I must not dissipate spiritual energy. Simplicity can be understood in one way as the refusal to dissipate. It is holding out against fragmentation. Simplicity holds the center against the impulse to go off in all directions, scattering your energy as you go. The phrase we use to describe this in rural areas is "like a chicken with its head cut off." Simplicity is focused. Where our treasure is, there our heart is. Our heart is where we live and love and discover the magnificence of revealed inner treasure. Simple living goes straight like an arrow. It seeks the center. It won't tolerate the clutter that keeps us from understanding. It clarifies the center, the real meaning of life.

Discipline

Simplicity is not easy. It requires discipline, something our culture does not like. In our orientation toward instant gratification we feel we cannot hand ourselves over to the time and effort it takes to give something space to develop and grow.

We can learn from nature. Pregnancy is a whole plan of discipline. The sperm meets the egg but then the laws of growth, the discipline of time takes over. It takes time for human life to develop. Normally that happens in stillness, darkness, and quiet. In an infinitely complicated fashion, a child comes into being. Nine months of waiting. The mother often is required to endure morning sickness, a rapidly changing and ungainly body that grows as it makes space for another. The mother must expand, create space within herself, almost a paradigm of generosity on the outside of the womb. It is difficult, requiring self-denial, patience, and love. Women have told me they are more contemplative, more mindful while carrying a child. How could they not be?

We hate but need real discipline in our society. Yet we will get no great beauty in life without it. We can't even wash dishes well without discipline. It takes ten times more discipline to use a dishwasher than it does to wash them in soap and water yourself, because it is so complicated to keep clearing and sorting and rinsing, etc. It can be much simpler to decide to wash the glasses in soap and water. Everything can take on a kind of ordered beauty.

Discipline is utterly necessary for spiritual living. It is necessary to rear a child. Why do you think parenthood is so difficult? It is beautiful and wonderful, but the discipline required—of patience, of waiting, of understanding requires extraordinary love and attention, consciousness, care, and time. Discipline means we wait for the child to progress at his or her own rate. We also have to pace ourselves. We need to apply the strength and order that goes with making something happen.

I found that teaching demanded great discipline. I loved school all my life. I had few great teachers. I had mostly ho-hum teachers all the way through school, but I did not have ho-hum parents. They would not let my ho-hum teachers dominate me or extinguish my love for learning.

When I was teaching in high school, I remember deciding I needed daily discipline to make sure I only taught one idea during a period. It took a lot of discipline not to dump a lot of things on the children they couldn't get. It took discipline not to run at my own pace and make a good show of getting things done. I had to make sure that at the end of 55 minutes no student left without learning the one thing I wanted to get across. If they could get five things a week, twenty things a month, I would be satisfied. I had to be centered and creative. It took a lot of energy to keep coming back to my single point.

It was thrilling to see how my discipline worked with the class, how it called them to their capacity for learning. My discipline moved into the lives of my students. My excitement and enthusiasm for learning moved into my students. I'm not sure how many facts they retained, but many caught the excitement and adventure of learning. Delight in living is more caught than taught.

The fruits of discipline are wonderful. They may be obvious in areas like sports, music or study; but also consider personal relationships. Holding your tongue, thinking before you talk, or listening with full attention can make the difference between sweet care or a careless cutting comment.

Some people hate discipline. I don't think many find it easy to cheer for it. What we do understand—and I know you've experienced it—is that when discipline comes from a heart of love, when it's understood as a gift, not imposed as a burden, we begin to love discipline, too.

Discipline comes from loving reflection. It's participation, rather than an imposition of some kind, like enforced obedience. Obedience can be a kind of discipline when done right. When I tried to understand the passage, "Be it done unto me according to your word," I was a bit afraid. It called for such a full response to mystery, to what I might not understand. I finally understood that as a human being I hardly create anything. Maybe nothing. I think I'm creative, but I'm only responding according to how I've been created. I'm a creature first. Always. Every creative act I do comes from this gift of life that comes to me from others. I learned we do things that may even appear proud but if it comes from a humble, honest heart, it is simply true.

I had a problem when I began public speaking. People would clap wildly for what I said. Sometimes they even jumped to their feet. That made me nervous. I appreciated it, but I didn't think I was that good. I was somewhat ashamed at the delight I took in their applause. I pondered it. People's applause concerned me for several years. Then one day I got an insight. They were not applauding me. They were applauding themselves. I learned that if what I said called and inspired them in their hearts, they would really applaud. But if I said something they disapproved of, or disbelieved in their hearts, their applause would be reserved. What did this mean?

They applauded what they knew in their hearts, their best selves. All I did was supply a fresh way of saying what they already understood. Once I understood that, the more they applauded, the better I liked it. The more stamping and clapping, the happier I was because within me I was saying, "It's what's in you that you are applauding. It's what you recognize as good and true within yourself. It's not me. I'm a little instrument. It's yourself in new language that delights you." That was a freeing discovery. When people would compliment me on my talk, I always knew the right response. "You're a great listener." They would say, "I loved your ideas." I could say, "You inspired me by the way you listened."

And that was the truth. That understanding freed me from fretting. I handed the result over to God while I prepared the best I could and then turned it loose.

I'm trying to give you an example of what is central to discipline. Any kind of discipline demands that you go to the heart of the matter. Discipline rids us of superficiality. We have to understand what something is all about. I had to discipline myself to keep probing for what applause meant or I would have been dealing superficially with it for thirty-five years. The discipline bore fruit. I just love it when people appreciate what I say. (I do have to be alert to see how objective they are. I can't soft-soap or seduce them by tailoring my message to what they want to hear).

When people tell me, "You're going to talk an hour, set your fee," I never do. Why not? I want to be free to say any darn thing I think I should say. If there's a fee, I might be a little beholden to whoever writes that check without even realizing it. I like to keep free. I think some people have cut down the size of the check because of what I said! They primed me to talk along one line and I chose another. I may have been well-received by the audience, but it was not comfortable for the check-writer, so my fee shrunk accordingly. When I see a smaller check, I know I am right to choose freedom over obedience to their wishes.

If we could only appreciate the relationship of discipline to freedom! Discipline is never for the sake of mere order. Discipline is never its own reason, it has no end in itself. It's never just to establish authority. Discipline is about inner spiritual power, it's about learning to control in one area so you can expand in another. If you can't discipline yourself to study, you will never have the thrill of discovery. Both learning and controlling are part of the meaning of discipline.

My father taught us the discipline of language out of love. He loved us and he loved language. He was an amateur etymologist. His tongue rolled around words with such delight that you would think you were sailing the high seas. He would ask us a question like "What is a beautiful word you've heard lately?" just to wake us up to listening. I remember one day I had this beautiful word I'd heard. I was waiting for Daddy to ask so I said excitedly, "I have one. Linoleum!" My brothers burst out laughing. They said, "Daddy, she thinks our kitchen floor covering is a beautiful word." Daddy said, "Well, let's say it. What's beautiful about the word?" I said, "It sounds like a song singing itself." My dad rolled the word around on his tongue several times and said, "I think she's right, boys. It's a beautiful word." I was elated.

The discipline of words came from our father's focusing attention on words. He'd say, "Listen. Study. Go look it up. Where does that word come from?"

I learned early to go to the dictionary. I tried it recently with the word "miracle." I can't tell you what the fifty or sixty definitions and ways of under-standing and using and defining miracle meant to me after that dictionary check. I thought it would take a minute to look it up. It turned out to be a whole evening of reflection.

When I was still a young sister I was on stage with Jesuit Bill Callahan. We were speaking to an audience of about a thousand Franciscan men and women. One man stood up and asked, "How can one really live simply?" It was a great question. Bill answered by saying, "I can give you an infallible plan for living your life simply." I sat with him on stage, and as he spoke, I memorized what he said I repeated it to myself, until I had it right. For two years I practiced it. It worked. It was possible. Here was an adult program that worked. He mentioned several areas we need to look at. Bill mentioned five areas. I added one more: work. This book tries to give you a program based on his original statement and a way to develop it in such a way that you can begin to look at your life in all of these areas. The program discusses material things primarily but only as they relate to your freedom of time, movement and ease in living.

So we begin by reflecting on our experience of what goes from need to luxury, and we make choices. Callahan outlined a program that is kind of a compact way of calculating and seeing our needs. This helps us determine what is useful, but not necessary, what we prefer, and what is sheer luxury. I have developed this information into a plan for action.

Consider the major areas of your life that involves material things. I find these six areas quite comprehensive:

1) Food
2) Clothing
3) Shelter
4) Work
5) Transportation
6) Recreation

In each of these areas we have four levels to consider: i) Need, ii) Help, iii) Preference, iv) Luxury.

The need level is basic for health and security. It is to have enough, or to have what is adequate. Basic is the word. The next level is to have what is helpful, what enhances or adds usefulness, or variety or comfort. The third level has to do with personal choices or preferences. These are not necessary and may not even be helpful in the utilitarian sense, but they delight, please or give us pleasure and satisfaction. The fourth level is luxury. This item is added to, or included, because it is extravagant, celebratory, or even merely ostentatious. It says "extra, abundant, the best." The Cadillac—in a car, a wheelchair, or cooking utensil.

Food

L et's begin with the first area of concern—food, because it is so important. We've had so many suggestions from doctors, pharmacists, herbalists, and alternative medicine practitioners telling us how to eat. We're constantly told that this or that is good— this or that is for us. Then two years later the opposite information comes along.

But there are some basics we learn by living. What do we need to be healthy? What makes us high-energy people? What keeps us from obesity? What helps us move with agility and grace? What keeps us mentally alert? We know we need to attend to our diet. We have to be informed. We need to educate ourselves, we need to weigh options. We know we have to eat. This is how we fuel these wonderful bodies of ours. We need to attend to what is necessary for good health. We have cultural and family histories.

What do we really need for a basic healthy diet? The same we hope for every person in this world—all the children, all those who suffer malnutrition because they don't have basics. We don't have to set out a diet as such, just say "What food do I need each day to keep me healthy?" We have to contend with advertising. It seeps in from all sides—TV, billboards, and magazines. It's plastered on the subway walls, on the backs of buses; it's on little napkins from the airlines. Every medium tells us what to eat. We have to be pretty calm and centered to decide for ourselves what we need.

Let's say we decide, "I need some grains." We get these mostly through breads and cereals. We decide we need cereals. How many cereals do we need stacked on our shelf? Often at places I go to work they say, "The cereals are in here." They open twin doors. I see about twenty brands of cereals in front of me. Every kind of bran flakes, not just one or two. Some have nuts, others fruits, others both. Some will have millet added, others have some other special ingredient. All the boxes will be half full. So if we say we need cereals, we may have to say, "Do we need to try every cereal advertised?" Do we need twenty brands open at one time or could we get by with three or four cereals that meet our basic needs? I offer this as one little area as a good place to start to practice simplicity.

We should decide we need fruit. We'll have to decide if we're going to get fresh or canned or dried or frozen. How much do we need for simple living so we're not always shopping where we're being tempted to buy with our eyes instead of just meeting our needs? Vegetables. Protein sources. Consider all. I am not a vegetarian, though I eat little red meat. For two years I was a strict vegetarian. I found I spent more time shopping and preparing, spent more money and less pleasure eating. So I changed and found a better way for me.

How many times a day shall we eat? How many times a day will we allow ourselves to snack? Are we going to allow ourselves useless snacks while we're trying to develop a global consciousness? We can't satisfy ourselves with every trivia in the snack world if we're concerned about those starving. We have to have a nice blend of common sense and Christian compassion. What we do in our personal life does make a difference on the planet.

The spiritual task is to discern between real needs and the extras. We don't need the extras. So we don't put Cokes and snack food down as a need. They're not. Some may need it as a help if we're addicted, but it's not a need. Include fasting in your consideration of food. We'll give special attention to that later.

Make a list. Keep it in front of you. It may be in your computer, your notebook, on the refrigerator or anywhere. Clarify your needs so you can approach simplifying your life with some intelligence and sense of reality.

Look at that list and say "In addition to these needs, what really helps me?" Here's where you'll add a few of these extras.

Besides the functional extras, there are some preferences. No, we don't need whip cream on our pie (at least not every time!), but if it gives you enough pleasure, enough delight, if it fills your mouth with ecstasy, have a little once in a while. Now it is a treat, not routine. This is not a need, not even a help, but a preference. Preferences should be occasional.

If we're living the gospel, we don't get every need, every help, every preference, every luxury met. If we don't deny ourselves, we're not living in an awareness of the rest of the world and the situation of the people around and beyond our neighborhood or *cul de sac*. There is a world of not having enough, that lacks the basics. We reinforce our blindness when we buy and accumulate what we don't need, what isn't particularly helpful, what should be occasional. Luxury is an occasional boon, not a constant indulgence.

When Bill Callahan told us about this program, he said, "In examining our needs in the light of the gospel, we find this: if you have all of your needs met, all of your helps met, most of your preferences met and most of your luxuries met, you are not living a gospel life. You are blind to the real world, especially the poor."

We can't saturate ourselves with what other people need for basics and still be living a gospel life. We never really heard that passage "If somebody has no coat, give him yours and your shirt as well." We didn't really hear those messages if we fulfill every eating desire. It doesn't take long or seem hard to understand this process, but you may find some real emotional blocks as you try to carry it out, especially in this area of food. Mostly in our society, we eat too much.

Clothing

Now, let's turn to clothing. I was speaking with a friend recently, and he said that when new houses are built these days, the great concern is closet space. He said almost always one of the first questions is, "How much room can we have for all of our clothing." "How many extra little doors and spaces." He said they really want a warehouse within the house.

What do we have in all these closets? Primarily clothing, but we also stack the shelves with a lot of other things besides. We glut them with everything from last year's Christmas decorations to clothes we bought for next year because it was on sale. (It's four sizes too large but somebody may grow into it!)

When we look at our basic clothing needs, we ask the same question. What do I really need? As a Franciscan sister, my clothing needs aren't the same as those of a married woman. I don't have any man to please. I don't have any family to pass judgment on whether I look contemporary or stylish or really "with" whatever modern phase we're going through. I'm freed from that. And I must say that is a great joy in my life, to have a few basic things and to not care, as long as I'm appropriately and cleanly dressed. I don't wear what other people give me if it doesn't fit my lifestyle. I don't let people dress me according to their needs or preferences or opinions. I make my own choices. We have to educate all of our friends and the people we work with so they promote our choices instead of trying to subvert them. They are apt to try to water down our desire because we may threaten their lifestyle.

I don't care what other people think. But a woman may have a husband who needs to maintain a certain level of dress because of his position. This can be done simply, too. How many fur coats do you need to maintain status? How many coats do you need to take you through one winter? How many sweaters do you need?

I've been to people's homes where the parents have four or five children who have left the nest. Many left their bulging closets behind. I've never seen one of those closets empty or even meagerly packed. Either the children don't take their stuff with them and keep bringing more home for the parents to store, or the parents begin to take over closet after closet. This one is for Spring clothes, this is for the Fall, this is Summer, this one is Winter. These are dress clothes, these are sporting clothes, these are swimming togs. Suddenly the house becomes a department store with every empty bedroom serving as a supply center. I have hardly ever opened a closet door when people have said, "Use this bedroom" and found even a hanger or two. I usually settle for backs of chairs because there aren't any extra hangers. Why? Everything is loaded down with clothing.

On the closet floor are usually twenty to sixty pairs of shoes. They're stacked high, in boxes and compartments and they've been there for years. Wedding shoes, snow shoes, sporting shoes, dress shoes, and work shoes. Shoes people couldn't get their feet into now if they wanted to! Sort them out. Give them away. Throw them away—but make decisions other than "Keep 'em!"

Some clothes are merely an act of hope. I've seen dresses hanging in closets that the owner hasn't been able to squeeze into for twenty years. Yet it hangs there in case she should lose forty pounds. Sheer fantasy. Give them away before they disintegrate into dust.

It looks ludicrous from the outside and shows what packrats we are. It's sad, though, to see things stored that someone could use for warmth or variety or a decent wardrobe to go to a job. Here hangs a whole world of clothing. Here sits a store full of shoes that nobody needs, nobody uses and perhaps nobody could even identify if they saw them in another context.

Now back to the program. Look carefully at your clothing. What do you really need for around the house. Almost everyone I know has three or four outfits they prefer. These clothes may be shabby, dog-eared, and falling apart, but they keep wearing them and ignore a whole closet full of other clothes. If you love to wear those, don't keep the rest around. Well, maybe two or three.

Consider: How can you keep your work wardrobe simple? Can you keep your cleaning bills down? Can you learn to travel with a wardrobe that doesn't demand four or five suitcases? If you're going for a weekend, how many clothes do you need for several days? Where is your imagination? Where is your creativity? Where is your appreciation for the time you save if you have just one carry-on? Do you realize how much time it takes to check five or six bags? Some people check the bulky ones and then try to carry on some illegal ones besides!

Clothing seems to be able to multiply by itself. Like rabbits. You start with three sweaters, then one day you notice you have ten. You start with two coats, soon you have nine. Four pairs of socks become thirty. You need to look at what you need for your daily life congruent with your life and your work. Then distinguish between what would be an occasional need and what might be a luxury. The more luxuries, the fewer you should have if you want to live simply.

Let's put the tradition of the examination of conscience to a new use. Don't just estimate. Don't just guess or talk to yourself. I'd write it down. You're quite apt to be surprised. Check all the closets too, not just your main one if you have more than one. The great principle for doing this comes later.

Housing

Now on to housing. That's expensive. Many people would love to own homes but can't afford them. Where do you live? Housing tells us a lot about ourselves. Housing is a status symbol. Houses and cars are our two great status symbols. If we live in certain neighborhoods, we know our children will never be exposed to other cultures. We know they'll never have to look at different colored skin. We know that nobody takes public transportation, nobody walks to school, nobody plays in the yard except children that look just like ours.

Where we decide to live is part of the life-education into which we thrust ourselves and our children. If you want to live simply, in a poor area, you have to know these areas. These people have to "make do." The area may not be destitute, just poor but you'll find that getting basic needs met can be difficult. If you want to live with people like that, (or you have a vow of poverty like I do), you have to find them. Go lookin'!

It doesn't matter particularly where I live but if I come into town—this happened to me when I came here to Gallup (New Mexico)—wealthy people would say to me, "We know a few good houses. And you will get a good deal on rent." Where were they? In upper or middle class neighborhoods. Well-cared for neighborhoods. Safe neighborhoods. The people would appreciate me and my work. But this would limit my availability to the poor. For example, I sometimes wait table in the soup kitchen operated by Mother Theresa's Sisters. This morning, when I was waiting table, one of the Indian men said, "Do you live in this neighborhood?" I replied, "Of course. Where did you think I would live." He said, "There's a dentist who comes to wait on us, but we don't know where he lives." The house itself doesn't make much difference but the location makes a statement about who is welcome at your house. How much time do you have to spend looking after a property in a neighborhood that has grass and is landscaped. Every choice has repercussions. It's not that you want to look poor. I have some basic needs and I meet them. I need some medication. I get it. If I don't, I'm not effective in my work. But I make sure I meet those health needs in a way that will put me in contact with the poor. I don't go to doctor's offices with appointments that whiz me right in because I'm such a busy woman. And a Sister! There's a kind of statement we make by where we are and how we are where we are that has to do with availability and our readiness to identify. Well, then, you drive from your neighborhood and do what you can. But don't expect to have an identification if you can't live near the poor or smell the poor or know where they can live or not live, sleep or not sleep. If you don't have any knowledge of that yourself, then don't expect them to see you as one with them. The poor identify you. What matters is, are you just as available to someone with $100,000 who is suffering as you are to someone who has 100 cents. Simplicity cuts through it all. Live where you are effective and it is right for you.

The homes will be like the people. If you move into a poor home, you move in with certain understandings. When I moved into my home, I discovered it didn't have a washer or a dryer. Of course, I could have gone out and bought a washer and dryer. But in this little town where I live, laundromats abound. What would that tell you? It tells you many people don't have washers and dryers. In this little town near a reservation, the native peoples come off the reservation. They are lucky if they have electricity or water, let alone machines like dishwashers, washers and dryers which waste water extravagantly anyway. I meet everyone at the laundromats. They vie with the newspapers for local news.

What kind of neighborhood in which we choose to put our roots down will make three-fourths of our decisions for us. It chooses our comfort level, our neighbors and much of our lifestyle. If we say we want to live simply, but move into a sumptuous neighborhood, where all of the lifestyle is betterment over the next person, with luxury one can see outside and inside, then we can expect to be seduced. We won't fit in if we are not. We'll end up apologizing and making excuses. We make our choices in prudent freedom.

Jesus and St. Francis are related to the poor in the same way. They identified with them and their service came out of the midst, not from afar. People often say to me, "I can't live simply like that. I'm not called to live like that. Yet I would like to help the poor." Well, then, drive from your neighborhood and do what you can. But don't expect to isolate yourself and expect to know what real needs are.

I know a lot of folks who live in certain homes and say, "Well, this doesn't really fit my mentality, but this was given to me" or "this is owned by so and so and I got it cheap." I pronounce this a bunch of bunk. If you are trying to really live simply in a way that matches your conscience, just do it.

The more we have to explain to the poor why we live where we do, why we dress the way we do, the more we have to defend ourselves, the more we're getting a sign that we're out of sync with our heart. We're not in touch with the principles by which we want to live.

When we consider where to live, whether it is apartment, house, or land, we have to look at the rent, interest or mortgage that goes with it. The best question to ask is what frees us and what burdens us. I'll say it often. Freedom is central to what simplicity is about.

Work

W ork is my favorite area. Mother taught me all about work, so I have hardly ever worked in my life. In one sense, I've been working all my life, according to other people's standards, but very little according to my own.

In the Native American traditions and in the languages I've known, we didn't have a word for work until we met Europeans. We have a word for living and work is part of living. Everything is living. We never divide life into work and play and recreation and rest. We live, which includes them all. We do what we need to do to live. If we need a home, we make a home. But don't be in such a hurry you can't decorate it.

There's an old story of Wavoka, the Ute Indian. He was approached by an agent, who said to him, "Wavoka, you're a very smart Indian. You could influence all these native people around here. You could get them to fit into white society." Wavoka responded, "Well, what would you see as the plan?" The agent said, "The first thing you have to do is teach them to respect time. If they have a job in town, they have to be at that bus stop on time. If they don't, they won't be on time for work." Wavoka said, "Then what?" The agent continued, "Well, then they go to town, and they go to work. And they work according to the clock. They don't try to leave when they are tired, or sit down and rest in between. They work all the way through until the bus returns at night." Wavoka said, "Then what?"

The agent, now on a roll, said, "Then by working steadily, they begin to make money. They can save money and put it in the bank. Eventually they can build a house and buy their own car. They don't have to depend on that bus." Wavoka repeated, "Then what?" "Then, if they keep working, they'll earn vacations and they can take two or three weeks off every year. They can go out and fish and hunt and live out in the wilderness." Wavoka said, "That's what we do all the time now."

Evaluate your attitude toward work and time. If you can understand this properly, you should not stay with work that can not give you pleasure. I recently read a twenty-year study of how our DNA affected whether we felt happy in life. They were looking at 20,000 people. They studied what made them happy. What did they discover? They asked these individuals, "Are you happy?" "What makes you happy?" Then they asked four or five people close to them, "Do you consider this person happy?" "What makes this person happy?"

The results were revelatory. Everybody, without exception, who said they were happy, gave as their main reason for happiness a spiritual path. They either followed or were seeking a spiritual path. Having found a spiritual way of living, pursuing it or searching for it gave them their deepest happiness. This might or might not be connected with formal religion. A spiritual awareness and the sense that there is meaning and purpose seemed to be connected in every instance with happiness.

The second thing that made people happy was a relationship or relationships that were intimate and deep enough to satisfy their soul. They fulfilled their need for spiritual companionship. This could be in marriage or friendship but there had to be that capacity for intimacy. The intimacy can also be with God.

The third ingredient of happiness was work. They had satisfying work that fulfilled them, delighted them, challenged them, and called them. Their work enriched their relationships, filled their time with pleasure, and gave them meaning in their lives. They felt they were really giving something to the world.

The fourth ingredient was quite startling. This group did not have work they liked. But everything about their job except the actual work was satisfying. They loved the environment, the people, or they believed strongly in what they were doing. They didn't like the actual work but the other components made up for that. The fringe benefits—like family security and higher standard of living—made up for lack of real enjoyment in the work.

After work, people listed creativity and the ability to play as primary sources of happiness. By the way, their research showed that the genetic (DNA) factor was thirteenth down the list. We aren't just born happy, we achieve it.

I mention this in connection with work because I consider it all part of work. I don't consider myself a working woman. I do what I love to do. I take all the little burdens that go with it. When I go somewhere to give conferences or direct retreats, or participate in workshops, burdens go along. Travel itself may be one, preparation is another, as is putting up with a lot of things not of my choosing. But those are subsidiary and secondary. I focus on what I'm doing. I'm meeting wonderful people, people with yearning and desire and a hunger to make their lives better. Nothing is more thrilling than to be in a position to call people to their best, to teach them whatever one has learned. That is usually satisfying, even exhilarating and fruitful. That's my work. I often feel that if not one person got anything from what I said, or what I shared, I was always better myself for having to prepare and deliver it.

What we call work, which might mean a little effort, a little sweat, a little inconvenience or a kind of steadiness that we'd just as soon not give, is hardly work at all compared with the fruitfulness and the meaning and the way we can make the world better.

Daddy used to say to us when we were little, "Try many things, find something you love to do. When you find something you love to do, figure out how to make a living at it. Don't start the other way around, trying to figure out how to make a living. You'll never be happy.

Try to learn to take less money and be more satisfied with loving what you do." When I said I wanted to be a teacher, he said, "You'll never make much money, but it's a great life." I still feel that professions like teaching and nursing and child care—all the nurturing professions—are wonderful jobs, if you can call them that. To me these works of building up the world are great privileges.

Work can be a ministry or service. I have worked cataloging International Harvester tractor parts. I've waited table. I've worked at a switchboard. I've cleaned dirty toilets in motels and made beds. I've collected bills, which can be very uncomfortable. I've done a lot of business things from the time I was a child babysitting and then working my way through college. I've had experience in at least thirty different fields of work before I got into my main work of educating. I've always found service possible.

A teacher taught me the inner soul of work. I learned in the eighth grade that I could be more than a teacher. I could be an educator. I had a wonderful eighth grade teacher who said, "why not be an educator?" That opened my mind! I realized I could always be doing what I loved to do no matter how many roads I took if I understood it in the context of educating or serving all these wonderful people.

So whether I teach children to make a stew or talk to students about a poem doesn't really matter. Calling people to spiritual integrity is a continuation of that same process. It's all my personal work of educating. It's about the light of self-development and self-realization.

Look at your workworld. Where do you spend your time? At home? In an office? In a shop? On the road or in the air? I've worked in a shop spending hours showing panty hose to women. What matters is that we spend our energy bringing people what they need. In this case, my job was to give them satisfaction and help them spend their money well. While we're doing work like that, we're also engaged in human communication and enriching lives in a small way. We discover a tremendous versatility, delight and wonderment at the world.

Where is your workspace? For some, it's in an airplane. Some business people spend more hours flying and getting where they're going than they spend at their destination. They have to consider their work area their space on the plane as they go toward their actual job. Whenever I go out to lecture or to work around the world I have developed a mentality I call curb to curb. When I get off a plane and get to a certain curb, I enter that workspace. I've also been in a workspace preparing while I was on the plane. Whether I was sleeping or studying or reflecting or praying, I was preparing for work. But my workplace began at the curb I left. However I got picked up didn't matter. Where I stayed didn't matter. That became my workplace. Everything demanded my adjustment to that schedule. I adjusted to their mealtime, their workspace, their liturgies, their cafeteria hours. My workworld was constantly changing. That remained my workworld until I went back to the curb.

When I got to the curb, I entered my next workspace, whether it was another assignment or a few days at home where I combine rest and work. It was essential to have a workspace mentality that traveled with me so I wouldn't be irritated by delays, sitting in lines, waiting or listening to multiple announcements that my flight would not take off. I was forced into constant accommodations. I pre-empted them and accommodated myself; then used my time so I wasn't under stress. I didn't get unduly fatigued or irritated because things couldn't go my way. Things just can't when we're traveling and using other people's spaces.

Our workspace may be large. It includes time getting to and coming from wherever we're employed. We create an atmosphere when we enter our home or motel room where we have a little control. That's part of work.

Now, let's turn our attention to "things." In speaking of material things, we're talking about what we make, what is around us for us to use. If we understand the value of these things, it is to help us along our journey and help us discover the full meaning of life. What things do you need for your work? You'll have basic needs. What are they (as distinct from wants and luxuries)? Do you need a typewriter or a computer? Maybe some things aren't strictly needs, but they are great helps. We need some helps—at least I've experienced that in our computer world. Once we get into computers and become fascinated with this whole electronic world, our needs and helps begin to multiply.

I know people who say about things like electronic games, "Well, I don't need this, but it is so much fun." Sometimes they'll say, "I never need this computer at home" but they have a whole room devoted to backing up what they have at the office. You don't have to be too bright to know you don't need all of that, so when you're cataloging, that's not in your need category.

The workworld needs more things in the helpful category than the others. Efficiency makes life simpler, in a way. So in the helpful category we put those things that make us more efficient. In today's workworld, given the speed at which we need to communicate, "helps" that increase speed become needs. We have to understand fax machines and e-mail and websites. What really helps us becomes almost a necessity to keep competitive and really be present to today's world.

This takes a special evaluation, but let's just look at our desk. How much do we need? How much is clutter? How much do we collect? How much do we need to weed out every few months? I have a way of collecting pens, pencils and magic markers. Every three or four months I have to give three-fourths of the stock away to make room for what will accumulate.

If I don't move it, I have to store it. If I have to store it, I have to protect it. If I have to protect it, I have to pay for protection. The first thing you know, I've created a monster when all I needed to do was learn to simplify and to give away.

Work preference or luxury will differ from your diet luxury or your clothing preference at home. They all need to be watched but through different lenses. What do you need to do your work well? Get it, keep it in tip top shape, use it. If you find you don't use it, suspect it. You'll probably have to get rid of it.

I kept track of my travel for fifteen years and discovered I never traveled less than 125,000 miles a year. Often over, never under. That's a lot of travel. That is my work. I had to figure out a way to make this work comfortable. I've been doing this for thirty-eight years now. It's never been my so called "full-time job." It's just something I do on the side—constantly, but it connects with whatever else I do. If I'm teaching at a university or working in a parish or diocese, I'm always doing this work around it, which is this travel. It's a big part of my world.

The first year I traveled, the businessmen sat in the back. I was one of very few women traveling. The world wasn't full of mobile women. I was a non-smoker and a sister, so I was in a different category and had the first five or six rows to myself. I could use the whole row, even across the aisle, for my office. I'd put the tops down, create a desk or two and have my office on the plane. I got a lot of work done.

I walked back to the place the men were gathered and said, "It looks like I'm going to be doing a lot of traveling. What tips would you give me to help me travel stress-free? I want to use my time and space as well as I can." In five minutes, those men gave me an outline for traveling that I still use. They told me never to check a bag if I could help it. To this day I don't check baggage. They said, "Go with carry-ons, a couple of small bags you can manage." So I do that. If I'm to go for more than a week, I travel with two small bags, I call one my brain and the other my body. I keep my clothes in one and my paperwork and books, etc. in the other. If I have to check a bag, I check the body bag. It's lighter, but who cares if I lose a dress or something. But it is important to me I not lose my last thoughts or presentation material.

They said not to sit in the window seats. They're beautiful and comfortable, but you can't get out in a hurry. If you have tight connections, be on the aisle where you can make a quick getaway. You never have to wait for your luggage. A window seat can delay you ten minutes if the people in the aisle and middle seat don't want to move. This mobility can free you from all the stress and worry about whether connections are made or not. I've found that traveling light is freeing and brings with it a kind of elation.

So if we work at home or in an office or church, we need to look for a way to make our own space. Then guard it. If our bulletin board has things on it for three or four years, we'll just have to get a burst of energy and strip it clean. If we can't remember what's up there, we might as well take it all down and start over.

How can I simplify things so that when I come home I don't spend my first day—or more—cleaning clothes, picking up trash and de-cluttering. First, I give myself a half-day vacation. I am a bit devious in carving out this mini vacation. I don't tell people exactly when I'm leaving or coming back. I say when I will probably leave and I make it half a day early. I say when I'll probably be back and I make it a day later. I need to make room for my soul. Part of my work is to keep time to read and keep fresh and to know what's going on in the spiritual world and the political world so when I talk to people I know what I'm talking about. That demands the discipline of preparedness. I am not so important that I can afford to slough off the time needed for reading, prayer and preparation that is at the heart of what I talk about. Our concerns are unique. What concerns me might be just laughable to you. It is important to me and holds me to a simple path.

Structuring our work life according to need, help and luxuries is more difficult than it seems because we spend so much time working that we develop a relationship with these materials. They become like extensions of ourselves. Let's look at our structure lovingly but with a keen eye. I limit books with a vengeance, because they are a weakness for me.

Transportation

Transportation is big. This can be status. Plain ordinary ways of getting around can move up into a way of being elite. The first thing we know, even if we could afford a particular car or truck, we don't want it because it identifies us with a certain class. We take on a certain momentum. A specific car can become a goal rather than a means of motion.

If we travel by bus or train, commute or carpool, we should examine that and compare it with traveling alone. When I lived in California, the great push was to get people to carpool. Nobody wanted to carpool! They wanted to protect that part of their private world. Their private commute was their recreation. What they listened to, what they ate, what they did with their time alone in their car meant too much to people for them to give up that solitary trip.

Now that I'm out of the heavy city traffic here in the Southwest, I can get on the road, drive only a few blocks and be with sagebrush and see mountains. I have a sense of *elan* wherever I go. I feel in touch with nature. I can see clouds. I know where the Sun is all hours of the day. The space creates a different space. Travel merges with recreation. When on the road, I can come over a hill and see a hundred miles. Work? Never!

Where do you travel every day? What do you do with your time? Do you study humanity, deliberately sitting back and spending your time watching people, with all the weird and wonderful things we do? Do you try to get a certain amount of reading done or devote that time to rest?

I see families with five children who have four cars. Two for adults and two for children, one of which has reached the driving age. I just marvel as they tell me that they need all those cars. They could even use one more, they assure me. What is there about our lifestyle that our children think everything, including their getting to and from school and sports, has to be instantaneous. They do not ever want to have to wait. They must never be inconvenienced. They never join the common herd. Walk? To walk fourteen blocks to get some place is not thinkable. What are we doing to soften ourselves up like this? Our children expect to be waited on. As teens, they are waited on constantly. They just say they need a ride and expect it to be delivered, even if it's six blocks down the street.

Sometimes we have two cars for the parents to go in different directions to work, a van for family transportation, a car of lesser value for the kids to drive, and an expensive rugged vehicle for off-road driving. Something is wrong with our need to have that much machinery for so few people. We're burning an excessive amount of precious fossil fuel just to live. It is a destructive pattern. It pollutes and deprives us of oxygen that we need for life. We don't have a global view of our consumption patterns. We have little realization of our degree of spending. (We are now 5% of the world's population, consuming 82% of the world's raw materials). Our mindset finds it hard to understand that less can be more. Transportation would be an excellent place to start.

The fastest way to get over absolute dependence on a car is not to be able to drive. I don't mean not having a car. I mean inability to drive. After seven surgeries on my leg, for a while I couldn't drive. To have driven for fifty years, usually having had a car at my disposal, not having to ask whenever I wanted groceries and then all of a sudden to be dependent on everyone else did things to me.

First, it made me very economical. I didn't need a fourth of the trips I used to take. It becomes obnoxious to keep asking. I realized how much time and energy I consumed. It put me in touch with my limits, physical limits. If I had to take a taxi, then I'd have to plan for that amount of money. I was suddenly thrust into a world that others have to live in all the time. It is possible to grow through the experience, even if it is difficult.

I've always planned my dwelling close to transportation. I've always lived close to a bus or train. I've always wanted alternatives to a car. You'd be surprised how often a person needs them. Now if I become dependent on other people, I can't get around the way I used to, then I come home to who I really am. We are all dependent creatures, only the degree of realization sets us apart. We are dependent on a force, a presence, a person beyond ourselves. We need, as a human being, to lean on someone who won't desert us, and someone whose power is immanent.

Recreation

The next area may make you smile, because one of the most expensive things in America today is recreation. It takes so much money to have a good time! It takes so much equipment to dress for having a good time! It takes such expensive gear to get to where we want to go to have a good time!

What do we really need to recreate ourselves? How self-fulfilling are we as a person or family or community to entertain and delight and amuse ourselves? Do we all have to be off in our own private expensive world to have a good time? To recreate ourselves? How much are we, really, in touch with creation and recreation? Do we know Mother Nature? Do we know our own backyard or our own plants in our own house?

How much can we do that doesn't cost money? Are we buying and selling and following every advertisement and every tilt of promotion? What can we do that is satisfying and delightful—and free? Or at least inexpensive. Maybe movies can be considered a luxury.

To habitually spend all the money for recreation that we might budget for other things is just amazing. I read that with all our credit card debts the two things we run up the most debts for are clothing and entertainment. You'd think those would be the two areas we could control easily, yet we go into debt extensively. So let's look hard at our recreational needs.

Maybe a book won't do it for you today in this computer age. Maybe you need music for recreation. But do we need all of the latest equipment to satisfy our musical needs? Or are some rather superfluous? Perhaps we could appreciate the best stereos in public places. You'd be surprised at how much good music you hear sitting in a mall. (You also get free heating and free entertainment (people-watching) while there.) Malls have lots of money, so they use good stereos and we can get free symphonies.

These are the major areas you need to look at. Write things down. Take inventory. Pray. Prayerful discernment is needed to decide what is need, help, preference, or luxury. Maybe you could begin by reading Matthew, Mark and Luke all in a row and see if you can pick up attitudes that Jesus promotes. He talks a lot about money and possessions, having and storing and saving and cheating to get. Read the gospels through that lens and see what Jesus teaches you. You'll find forty or fifty references just to "things, money and stuff."

Worrying about things is a frequent theme. Three or four hours of reading might give you a gospel mentality about what you might do.

Inventory

Now let's get practical. Theory without practice gets wearisome. Enter simplicity. That's how we bring the theory and practice of discipline together.

Let's begin with Bill's way of making it happen. After we've set out these major areas that comprise our life, break them down into the four categories:

needs, helps, preferences, and luxuries. Write them down. Actually make lists. Take notes on what you're thinking. In business it's called taking inventory.

Every business has to take inventory. They do it periodically—some daily, some monthly, some yearly. Depends on the nature of the business. What do I have? How much space do I have? Where is clutter? When do I have to have a sale? A giveaway?

Taking inventory is a good time to introduce you to the great Native American spirituality practice of giveaway. The principle of giveaway is to always have your hands open to a gift. Either you're giving it or you're receiving it with the possibility of giving it again. You never receive a gift with a clenched hand. If someone hands you a gift, you never put your fingers around it. That would say, "I'm holding." Hold it in an open hand to look at it. As you look at it, you wonder if it should rest with you or if it should rest with someone else. You have been listening and you know the needs of many, so that gift may come to you with the sure message that it is to be passed on. That's a spiritual understanding of recycling.

The open hand is to keep one ready to share. Doesn't that remind you of the story that keeps multiplying itself through all four gospels—the multiplication of loaves? The little narrow-minded disciples are concerned about what they will have for themselves. Jesus insists that they share. The miracle is how much is always left over. There's never just barely enough to go around. There's always an abundance. That's what simple living is about. You think you are talking about one thing and in your very hand it is multiplying itself. Suddenly you're collecting the resources that go with your real concerns in life.

Giveaway is unique to Native American traditions. It has some unwritten but clearly understood rules or principles. First, any gift given has more power if it is never wrapped up. It is not put in a box, or put in a paper or tied into secrecy. A second source of power is your own creation. If you have made it, it has more power. To take a gift you have made and hand it over, without any tissue or box between you, is almost like communion in Native spirituality. You create a flesh to flesh connection. And whenever you give with that kind of wholeness it is understood that the gift is truly, freely yours. It is nothing that you must hold on to or you must display. With the gift goes the smile that says the receiver may give it away. It is yours to receive and yours to give.

That Native American traditional quality of nonpossessiveness, of not grasping, is crucial. If the original giver sees the gift elsewhere, that expands the heart. The giver gives so freely that the giving continues. There is no hurt feeling if the gift is given further. Instead there is a joy that along with the gift went an experience of expansiveness for the receiver. The magnanimity of the receiver, nourished by the original gift, allowed the receiver to pass it on.

The reception of gifts helps you understand how much you want to give away. You discover the pleasure of sharing rather than the burden of caring for things. Sometimes people will give me gifts and they say, "I want to give you this for yourself. You have to keep it for yourself." At that moment, we have to teach people that that's not the way we live. We simply have to say, "I can't keep it for myself. If someone else needs it more, or there's an appropriate place for it or it will make someone else happy, I can't hoard this in a pocket or on a shelf." I can't even keep it on my windowsill if it will make someone else happy.

We can violate the spirit of inventory, too. Taking inventory can just be a signal to stock more. These items now need more shelves and more space! But if that inventory is inspired by magnanimity, by a sense of giving and generosity, there is no limit how fruitful it can be. That fruitfulness doesn't come from a dusty shelf, it comes from the flow of the spirit.

Inventory for a good businessperson is never simply replacement. When we come to replacement after inventory, instead of accumulation, we come with a different understanding. We have freely decided what we need, or helps or will give us an occasional lift. But we don't want to be encumbered. We are not interested in expanding our material world. We're interested in the flow of spiritual energy and the wonderful gifts that come from that.

Take inventory carefully. From then on, if the inventory matches what you have disciplined yourself to have, simply replace what's missing. If nothing is missing, you do not add. The principle is replacement, not accumulation.

But, because we are free in spirit, we give ourselves a little grace, a little leeway. You who know me know I don't have many clothes. I love clothing. I took a minor in fashion in college. I wanted to be stylish. I also took a minor in home decoration for the same love of beauty. But I have a vow of poverty and I need a lot of time to spend on study and preparation. So I don't allow much inventory of clothing.

What could be a pitfall for me with my values? I'm an educator, a teacher, interested in learning. What do you think I lust after? The availability of books! I have to look at the real world. Clothes are not a problem. Books are. They always have been. I just love them! I want them. I want my own. I would like to build a separate building just for a library of beautiful books. But if I want to live in freedom, I have to discipline my love for books.

Here's how I curb my appetite for books. I asked myself if I were on a desert island, what books couldn't I get along without? I decided I need six books. I just have to have a good New Testament translation, a full bible, a wonderful concordance. (Mine is the great Cruden's Concordance, a gift from my motherhouse library. He went insane compiling it and somehow it seems worth it. All other concordances derive from his.) Those three books are fixed. I keep them permanently. Then I need three books to inspire me. Those might be a spiritual read, Rilke's or Emily Dickinson's poetry or something I find exceptional. These could rotate, but I keep them for a long time until I have absorbed them. I may even return to one after having exchanged it.

I need books for what I do for a living. I speak to groups about a lot of topics. I talk about simple living, Native American spirituality, prayer, spirituality, peace and justice, and women's issues. So I need a small library that goes with my work world. Those books help me be more efficient so I don't have to run to the library every time I have to check a reference. If I work in various areas, how many books do I really need? I whittled it down to thirty-six.

So now I have six personal and thirty-six work books. If the work changes, so do the books. What if publishers send me a book to review? Or what if somebody gives me a great book and I've already got my thirty-six? My way of handling this is to give myself three days of grace. I either read it and give it away, or keep it and get rid of another book. I must confess, this rule is so important and I am so selfish that sometimes I stay up all night to finish a book before I have to give it away.

I learned this from my mother. My mother and father each took one night a week "out." We always knew what my mother did from five in the evening until the next morning when she turned out the light to get up to make coffee. She read all night. She read *Gone with the Wind* in one night. I know, because I checked it out of the library and took it back the next day. The librarian challenged my bringing it back. "She just took it yesterday! She can't have finished it!" She took the book over to my mother and said, "Did you really read this? All of it?" When mother told her she had, she inquired further, "Well, when did you sleep?" My mother told her that she didn't. The librarian was shocked. She said, "You mean you read all night? If I did that, I'd drag around all day." My mother informed her that's exactly what happens. "I drag around all day, but I've got a book in me forever." My mother understood that discipline and that simplicity.

I have to count my books once in a while. I have to take inventory every few months or new ones will slip in. It's a constant discipline. People give me books and if I start making exceptions for myself I'm violating my own discipline, my own real insight that I need to limit books in order not to be cluttered in an area dear to my heart.

Perhaps this is how the canon of the books of the bible came to be. The church leaders had to decide what was inspired and what was not and they had to limit how many books they could declare worthy of being considered inspired. After all, what if we had

1,200 books instead of seventy-two in our bible? Or what if it could go on forever? Hmmmm . . . .

Because books are so important, I frequently wonder, what happens if I lose my eyesight? No more reading. I hope I already have enough books in me to make up for that deficit. I hope I have ears so I can listen. To make sure a supply of books exists for people who cannot see stays full, I read and record books for other people as a hope it will promote my ability to hear other people's gifts someday if I can't see. I record for the blind six hours a month.

After you've cleared what your categories and discipline say you have to clear, you may feel a little fainthearted. That happens. We get a burst of generosity followed by a wave of remorse. If you feel ambivalent about some stuff, set a few things aside and mark them tentative. If you think this is easy, let me share with you that it usually takes people about two years to really discover how much they really need in each category, what tends to accumulate, and to identify their personal fears and their own proper level. Once you get that level clear, write what you are going to do to simplify in each area. From then on, allowing a few days of grace, you must impose sanctions on yourself if you violate your levels. That means every three or four months you check yourself, especially in your acknowledged areas of weakness. I don't have to check many areas out anymore, but I simply must check my books. If you violate your principles, give some clutter away. Get into the habit. This isn't just a garage sale. We don't allow ourselves extras "just in case." We don't pander to our weaknesses. The "just in case" mindset is common if you've been raised by someone who lived through the Depression. Watch out for it.

How do you get rid of these things? Give them away. If you just don't have the heart to give them away, you might have to bury or burn them—something drastic. You may have to have a bonfire in your backyard. Invite the whole neighborhood and tell them to come to your burning party. Stand by your possessions that you are too weak to give away and too concerned about to throw away. Just say, "Burn, baby, burn." You have to start fresh.

When we pare ourselves down to our proper weight and level, after a year or two it becomes natural to keep turning things over by giving things away. We develop a sharper eye for who needs our excess. We learn how to give our material goods away so that it means something to us and the receiver. We become experts in a new kind of recycling. We find ourselves more open to the needs of the people. It becomes as difficult to accumulate as it once was difficult to give away.

There is only one drawback. We can spend so much time giving stuff away that the art of giving eats up our time like hoarding did. We can become more efficient at that, too, though. Just kidding. Giving away is a happy problem. Just make sure you give yourself two years to get in shape! I did this thirty-two years ago. I sat down and planned it. It took me two years to hit my stride and I've been re-evaluating every so often for thirty years. It isn't a burden. If I don't get a lamp that I think I need, maybe I just don't need it. We all have gradually adjusted to expecting to acquire what we think we need immediately. Waiting is a salutary discipline in itself.

A Light Heart

Simplicity works best with a spirit of play. One purpose of simplicity is to have a good time. You'll discover an inner extravagance and you'll surprise yourself at your own sense of adventure. Call yourself to do things that you've never tried before. You'll be amazed at how much fun you have and how much freedom simplicity gives you. You'll experience a kind of joy of heart.

I've saved the best for now. Simplicity is a natural preparation for prayer. Simplicity will lead you to prayer. It creates an inner awareness of gratitude for the material and spiritual gifts you have. It creates time and space for prayer. I believe that simple living and prayer go hand in hand. After the real but light-hearted effort of simplicity, we often receive the gift of deepened prayer.

As we begin to limit ourselves, some of us may feel a cold shadow of fear. What if I'm deprived? What if I run out? If you practice this and begin to share, you'll discover that you always have more than enough. You always have overflow. Jesus frequently told the disciples to stop fretting. "Therefore I tell you, do not worry about your life, what you will eat, or about your body, what you will wear" (Luke 12:22). Wherever Jesus went, he created abundance. He healed the sick, cast out demons, filled fish nets to overflowing and fed 5,000 people out in the desert. In the parables and actions of Jesus, we meet a cosmic extravagance. The messianic age is one of abundance, as the prophets foretold. My favorite prophecy of abundance is at the end of the book of Amos. "The time is surely coming, says the Lord, when the one who plows shall overtake the one who reaps, and the treader of grapes the one who sows the seed; the mountains shall drip sweet wine and all the hills shall flow with it" (Amos 9:13).

It will happen in large and small ways for you. You'll see it just when you run out of milk, you'll be amazed at who stops in with something. You've given too much of something away and it comes back to you in another form. You find yourself busy handing off what comes in. Your back door is just as busy as your front door. And when you keep them both open, the breeze is terrific! It's that feeling of open exchange that makes us feel free and exultant. It's enough to make a person dance!

It's like this. We give away our coat. Then we lose our shirt to someone else who needs it terribly. Whereupon we discover it's too hot for either one and we need the sunshine. The rub is this: we won't know it unless we experience it. To begin requires Faith. Otherwise it just seems as foolish as the cross. But once we experience it, we are on guard all the time for experiences of losing and gaining. We'll never want to be sucked back into the greed derby again. We can be sucked back in of course. We have to be a little careful.

It helps to have friends or a community to support us. If we don't, our friends will draw us back into the accumulative lifestyle. When I first entered the convent, my brother, who had quite a bit of money, didn't really approve of my choice. He couldn't send many gifts but at Christmas he'd always send the kind of gift that I had to deal with. He never sent me a simple gift. He'd send me an engraved dictionary or a watch specially embossed. The gift always said, "Oho, you have to keep this. There's no way you can give this away."

It tested my creativity. I couldn't have what he wanted me to have. He was trying to distract me from what I was about. Finally I just had to confront him and say, "Quit it. It just takes three times as long to figure out who gets that gift." He learned. We have to educate our friends.

Now if an older person gives me something he or she has made and I know it embodies time and effort, I wouldn't just give it to anybody. I would make sure I used it and appreciated it for a while. But I would also say, "After I've used it a while if I see someone who really needs this, you wouldn't mind if I pass it on, would you?" In my experience, they don't. So you're not callous or putting up a barrier to gifts. Some people do give quite unacceptable gifts. I say something like "What a wonderful gift, I know just who has space in their yard for this."

Try to call other people to generosity along with you. Sometimes, understandably, they're a bit reluctant. They pick out gifts that are expensive. Because the gift is costly, they expect us to keep it. We have to let them know, as tactfully as possible, that an expensive gift like this just doesn't fit how we're trying to live and would be a hindrance in our spiritual quest. "With the best of intentions, you would just encumber me with this gift." We perform a spiritual work of mercy by instructing them. We teach them how to help, not hinder us. But always remember:

what is not appropriate for one may be quite appropriate for another.

Discernment

These kinds of spiritual choices require discernment. What do we receive, what do we reject? We will not know how deep to cut our storage if we don't pray. We need an inner light because we must be guided by grace. This has nothing to do with looking poor or going around shabby. People assume it does. Some people ask me, "Do you want us all to live with ragged curtains and dirty windows?" No. I don't want anyone to live with anything dirty or raggedy. That's not the point. We're not talking about a poverty of deprivation. We're talking about less is more. We are talking about what is at the center of our life. I want you to have all of your needs met and then some. That's not deprivation. But true simplicity teaches us joy with less, and easy movement.

Discernment will show you the difference between frugality and stinginess. Stinginess is self-centered and pinched, just the opposite of the expansiveness of simplicity. We usually hoard out of fear, just the opposite of faith. Stinginess is selfishness, but simplicity is for the sake of real love for ourselves and others.

Frugality doesn't mean not spending. Frugality means a thoughtful economy. We're frugal if we use our time well. We're frugal if we cook with healthy materials. Frugality and simplicity or poverty of spirit all say limit, don't waste. Stinginess is just greed and usually clutters our lives. Frugality is a careful examination of the complexities of buying and selling and deciding how to remain free in this complex transaction.

I've worked with a group called Ministry of Money. These people have lots of money themselves or work with those who do. Part of their self-understanding is having an obligation to help people see where to use their money well, how to be good stewards. One thing struck me forcefully. I worked with one particular group. Three had earned their money. Several had made their money, lost it and made it again. The fearful people, who were guarding their money the most carefully, never lifted a finger to earn it. They had inherited it. I don't know the exact history, but most of them told me their money had been given to them by someone who made it off the backs of the poor. They often presented me with what to them was an unsolvable problem. "What shall I do? How do I know people aren't trying to use me when they ask me for gifts? How do I know people aren't trying to take advantage of me?" My answer is, "You don't. So get rid of it all. Then go earn a little yourself and feel what it's like to earn a living instead of guarding money that came to you through inheritance!" I tried to get them to see their money was mostly a burden. I suggested they set themselves up modestly and give the rest away. They were walking in fear and suspicion of everyone and they were not at all happy. Actually, I told them they had no right to the money. They were claiming it, but they didn't earn it, it wasn't good for them and it was controlling their lives. They were in such a quagmire, dealing with the money issues that they would be better off not having it. I told them frankly, "My mother could teach you a lesson. Go spend it all! You'll see what will happen. Things start coming back to you and the first thing you know, you'll have friends you can trust. People will have nothing to get from you."

Wealth does bring out the worst in some people. People take advantage of you; no matter what you have, they want it. I've had experiences of people doing that to me. No matter how tired I am or how hard I've worked or how generous I've been with my time, people want extra blood. They want to pick your brain until the last second. They don't care if you're exhausted or weary; if they paid you a little bit to come, they're going to use you up. One has to understand that that is abuse and you have to refuse. You have to not let people steal your gifts just like they would your money. But a sure way to not have people use you for your money is to not have any.

Integrated Prayer

These are hard decisions. We need to learn discernment. If we're used to only praying the rosary or just one kind of meditation we find a need to enlarge our prayer life. We begin to integrate our prayer with our decisions. Once we learn how to act, our hearts open to other possibilities. Our prayer becomes much more inclusive. Our prayer reaches out and adds another dimension to our decision-making. We decide what we must do in the light of what we discern God wants us to do. In John's gospel, Jesus said, "The Father who dwells in me does his works" (John 14:10). That's our ideal. We decide with the time and resources we have. As we learn to discern, we reach for the largest understanding of God with us. We now integrate our need for integrity and enlightenment into our prayer. Prayer becomes more fully integrated into our life. We may find in prayer for discernment we may be led to insights from other spiritual traditions. Perhaps a Buddhist or Taoist saying will occur to you. That's perfectly all right. What difference does it make? When the light comes to you in prayer, follow it.

Part of simplicity is a greater openness to truth. Once we have our inner freedom, we find ourselves more spiritually supple and we are able to absorb truth from more sources, sometimes not Christian ones. The insights from a solid tradition may far surpass our own individual and limited understanding. Our habits of seeing tend to be a bit too tightly focused. We need the expansion. We often overlook the truth that simple living opens to new wisdom.

But if we are hoarding even what insight we have, we tend to set up rules to hold our own precious truth. We develop strict rules, and because hoarding is done out of fear, we also trust very few sources. We seek enlightenment from only a few places. Our lives become small and sorry. But if we become simple, enlightenment comes from everywhere. Do you know the story of Balaam's ass? (Num. 22). The most unlikely place for enlightenment to come to Balaam was through his talking donkey, yet that's exactly what God chose for an instrument of revelation. So if God wants to get a message through to us, God can talk to us through the dog next door. Our job is learning to listen.

The Adventure of Faith

Simplicity is bracing and requires a certain spirit of adventure. Real spirituality involves some risk. For example, every spiritual tradition requires us to fast. Fasting has been recognized as a spiritual value for centuries. In our schema, this relates to the area of food, of course. To overcome fear and to increase awareness of our spiritual capacity we often profit from denying ourselves food. Fasting is not holy dieting and has nothing to do with losing weight. Fasting is more about this truth: if we have less, then we have more. So if we take less food, we have more capacity for spiritual hungering.

Let me recommend this ancient discipline of fasting to you. Put your toes into the cold water. Fast once in a while. It's good for us physically and spiritually. Take the chance. It's a biological expression of your willingness to expose yourself to deprivation. Kierkegaard, the great philosopher, tells a story about geese. They flew long distances over open water and came to this barnyard. There they no longer had to search for food. They were very well fed. Some really ate their fill and became very fat. But when the time came for the return migration, the fat ones couldn't make it. They were so heavy they couldn't clear the barnyard fence. Only the less glutted ones were able to make the flight home. The meaning is clear for us. We just can't fly in life if we are too encumbered. And encumbrance, as we have discussed, takes many forms. We need a slimming down in the spirit so we can move with generosity and grace and sometimes speed.

Inner Power and the
Spirit of Adventure

Once we discover that we have company on our journey, and that company brings with it a power that cannot be overcome, even by the natural disasters of this world, our faith and prayer life grows. Our actions change correspondingly. The stronger our faith gets the more we walk in it. Look for these signs of that faith. The first is an awareness of strength within ourselves, it is not from anything outside of us. It's an inner experience. It's a path of personal enlightenment telling us who we are. As this develops, one becomes aware that nothing in the world can overwhelm us. As our consciousness of this power far beyond ourselves reveals itself to us, we fear nothing, not even death or fear itself. As the great chiefs and churches have always said, we never really die. We don't cease to exist, we move to a new form. Life is changed, not taken away. Our freedom from fear grows out of this consciousness that we cannot be done in.

As we are carried by this power, it may look to other people like foolishness, but we gradually free ourselves from concern about their opinions. When we discover our own inner peace and happiness, our ability to laugh in the face of adversity, we become a bit embarrassed by how slow we have been in coming to this inner place. It's hard to accept how long it took us to understand the full meaning of words we have heard preached (and preached ourselves) all our lives.

This inner knowledge that we do not walk alone but are held by a wise and caring God is the ultimate reward for having acknowledged our dependence. Nothing can supplant or surpass this knowledge.

When we connect fasting with this desire for spiritual abundance, we discover its relationship to simplicity. Fasting is a face of simplicity. It makes space and place and heightens our desire to see God. Fasting and simplicity in general increases our capacity to experience spiritual abundance. Simplicity enables us to find largeness in each area of life—body, relationships, environment. We discover not only abundance awaiting us, but a vastness. There is space beyond our wildest imaginations. The more freely we move, the more we touch our limits and expand them. Because we have fasted, because we have denied ourselves in one form, we have created fullness in another form. It is a joy that surpasses understanding, much less articulation. We "get it," but there are hardly any words to describe it.

Children can be aware of the limitlessness of life, but frequently lack discernment. We need to learn the discernment, but never let go of that fresh vision of life without spiritual limits. Without the vision, we are old and small before our time. Without the discernment, we rush in where angels fear to tread. I remember when I was a little girl, not yet in the first grade. I loved swings. I'd go to the playground and watch people having so much fun and I would swing and swing. I would think, "Wouldn't it be a wonderful thing to be able to go over the top without falling out!" I never told anybody that because I knew that would be a rather daredevil thing to do. A terribly adventuresome thing! And I would be discouraged. But I kept asking myself, "Is it possible to pump so high that I could go over the top and not fall out and die?" I thought about it for a long time. My brothers would push me in the swing and they'd push me really high. They pushed me extra high one day and I decided I was going to try to go over the top. If I could go over fast, I could stay in that swing. I had secretly planned to do this. One day everything was just right. No wind. I was ready. I could feel the excitement. I rode a hearty push, gave a huge pump and went all the way up—and stopped dead center. Whereupon I fell down, crashed on the top of the bar holding the swings, fell further to the ground onto a sharp stone at the base of the swing. I suffered a big gash on my head from that stone. I bled all over. I was screaming at the sight of my blood and my brothers were terrified. They took me home. My parents chastised my brothers. "How could you let her do that?" They took most of the heat. It didn't turn out to be so bad after all, just bloody. So I decided I knew why I couldn't go over. So even though the word was "Watch her!" I knew I was going over the top again. I would wait until the furor died down and then I'd make my move. I knew what I didn't have. I didn't have the momentum. I needed more of a rush!

So in the fall, a few months later, I was out swinging. The wind was right. It was a nice day. The time was right. My brothers were pushing really hard and I was going higher and higher. But this time I had a different feel for how much momentum I needed. I gave it my most powerful pump. I went up and over! I made the full circle, came down on the other side unscathed. It was scary when I realized I had come down with a much shorter chain, but I had the most wonderful sense of accomplishment! I was hung up on the pole, but I was over! I had figured it out. I knew momentum was the key! I have to confess. I never tried it again. I never wanted to try it again. I never wanted to see if I could go over twice. I had reached my goal. That was enough. I still have a knot on my head, reminding me of the importance of discernment. To this day I take an enormous amount of pleasure in swinging. It is still a metaphor for going beyond established limits.

The adventure did something for me as a teacher. When students would come to me with wild ideas, with ideas their parents prayed they'd never have, I'd help them with the process of discernment. However,

I always respected that mysterious something in the human spirit that has to see how far it can go without getting too many lumps on the head. I think I have a deeper understanding of why people ride roller coasters and take daredevil leaps on motorcycles. I know why I had to spend three years learning to do the Commanche run: riding at high speed without a saddle, and disappearing, only to reappear on the horse. It isn't all stupidity or showing off. It has to do with the presence of the Spirit within us. We have an inner reach we must extend. We need to set a mark. It may be too high but in the effort, we find our heart. We are created for adventure and it is this spirit of adventure that simplicity nurtures. We have to live unprotected if we're going to really live. So I've always given students with wild ideas a second ear. I've always loved the free, foolish Francis of Assisi!

We're never beyond adventure. Because I travel so much, it was suggested to me that I have a credit card. People pointed to my extensive travel in many countries and put it this way. "We would feel safer if you had a credit card." I thought about that. I didn't think I needed a credit card. Sometimes when one makes decisions like that, people think you're a little fluffy, mentally. Sometimes people make decisions like that because they know themselves. They know their capacities. So I said, "All right. I'll get a credit card, but give me a few years to see if I need it. If it turns out that I'm living impractically, I'll get a credit card." Well, it's been thirty-eight years and I've never had a credit card. Yet, I do things that people say I should not be able to do without a credit card. I don't sleep in the street, I don't get rejected by motels, I've rented a car with $50 cash and taken it over the Canadian border. I experience that what we need is really an ability to relate to people. Most people would love to beat the system. People allow me to get along without the required card because they love to be an accomplice in something that is honest but thwarts the system. People have repeatedly let me bypass lots of paperwork, forms, requirements, office policies—and they've enjoyed it. I've had some wonderful experiences because I never had a credit card. Some look at this in disgust. You can say it is foolish. Perhaps, but there's an inner joy that has come from these foolish things that many people would never try. And I've lived a little more fully.

These things may look foolish, but so does simplicity sometimes. Most adventures are a little foolish. They are seldom required. Simplicity is an adventure. Simplifying your life in this streamlined manner gives you a kind of speed. You move like an arrow through dust and muck. It's not really foolish, it's just clean. Simplicity gives life a freshness and directness that enables you to go straight to the heart of things, like a child's observation that the emperor wore no clothes.

We have a fine example of simplicity in the story of David and Goliath. Goliath was a massive war machine in human terms—shielded, helmeted, protected in every way. He is a human metaphor for our Defense Department, looking after every need down to the twine of his sandals. David had a simple slingshot. No sword, no armor. And with a simple slingshot he did the impossible. He laid Goliath low. We have Davidic victories in us. We won't discover them unless we examine our fears and take off some armor. Some fears are legitimate but they need to be tested. Most people wear too much armor. Their armor is felt to be necessary because it is based on the fears of others. The government frightens us so they can have a huge Defense Department, our parents often carry fears from their childhood a long time ago. Prejudice against a people of color or origin is often simply our acting out of the fears of our parents. But perhaps the most frightening thing is our own imagination.

When I was a child coming home after dark, it was amazing how frightening ordinary things were. I had a vivid imagination and was correspondingly frightened. One time an old bulldog took a bite out of my little yellow ruffled dress when I was very little. I ran home screaming in terror, telling my parents I had been ripped practically to the bone. My dad looked and said I hadn't been bitten at all. He explained that the dog was old and had poor vision. When I turned quickly, he got confused by the wave of yellow ruffles and bit down on it. He had me go back and pet the dog and I was never afraid of it again. (I did, however, back away!) But I know I could have gone my whole life afraid of that or any dog.

We need to let go of the fears of our childhood. Paul writes, "Now that I am grown up, I have put away the things of a child" (1 Cor. 13:11). When we live simply, we find ourselves confronting these childhood fears, these borrowed and social fears. When simple living confronts these, we learn to discover what is true for us. What is true for you may not be so for me. I might never send you into a situation into which I would go freely. The opposite is also true. Each of us has our own experiences, inner truths and private limits that we need to test. I'm grateful that I'm a Franciscan sister, in a lifestyle that calls me to joyful freedom.

Prudence

Going over the swing was frightening because there was no middle ground. I either made it or I fell hard. Simple living is not that either/or choice. It allows us to calibrate our risks. It allows us to taste and test. We take a step and look around, then take another, like a deer entering a clearing. It's the knowledge of taking those steps and trusting them that finally brings out the abundance. We develop a great-heartedness in our own path. We know what we can do because we can practice. It's like learning to play the piano. We learn one note, then a few, then an octave. The first thing we know, we're playing. Then when we are ready, we can play with force and grace and ease.

Prudence isn't the same as caution. Sometimes it can look like you're not protecting yourself when you're really doing the safest thing. When I was out in Montana in some rather wild country we had an understanding that if we left the house and the weather was terrible, we didn't lock the door. We had no desire to keep anybody out. If someone needed shelter from that tough weather, they were welcome to it. Every so often we'd come home to find a sign that someone had made coffee, sat at the table and left a sign of gratitude. It might be a rock, or thank you note. We felt connected to this person in need. Our fears decreased because we weren't afraid of being robbed. We were comforted to know that if we were in bad weather, we could stop and find shelter along the way.

Bodily Spirituality

Some folks admire simple living. They tell me they want to simplify their lives. They would love to unclutter. They would love to walk freely. But they really don't want to do it because they don't do it. To live simply, we must take the actual steps. We must physically clear out the excess, you must take steps to prevent accumulation. We can't do it in our heads. Simplicity is not just an idea.

That means it walks around our home with us. It gets in our car and goes to work with us. It shops with us. Our body is in on the act. Our body wears the clothes. Our body eats. Our body fasts. Our body is a sacramental presentation to all who can accept that this is real, healthy, and whole. The visibility of simplicity makes it a witness and accounts for some of its influence on others. Simplicity is an inner harmony others can see.

I think this physical manifestation of simplicity is crucial. Thinking about simplicity can occupy us for centuries. Head trips never end. People can speculate forever about what can be done or what is possible and helpful. Jesus didn't speculate. He walked the streets. He got dusty, dirty and probably smelly. He was out in the sun. He appreciated a footwash so much that John records it.

Simplicity creates comfort for our bodies, but not waste. We can't live in air-conditioned rooms all the time. When we need only a fan and still insist on conditioned air, we waste precious energy and it doesn't make us any healthier. Why not learn to be quieter and slower when it gets hot? Learn to appreciate the cultures that have learned to live with heat. Perhaps we could learn to be more sensitive to our bodies, learn to sit still and meditate during those times of heat-enforced quiet. I'm reminded of a Papago story from their reservation in Arizona. They had watering holes called *chacos*. They were places their cattle would come to drink. The natives knew the cattle couldn't go without water longer than three days. No matter where they were, they'd come back to the watering hole on the third day. So their idea of a roundup was just to go to the watering hole and wait. They'd play cards, roll dice and just wait. They enjoyed each other and their games and as the cattle came, they sorted them out. They couldn't understand the anglo cowboys who rode the range in fierce heat, driving their horses to exhaustion hunting cattle who would come anyway if they just waited. But the excitement of saving time, looking busy and working hard was so important, they never did learn to let the cattle come to them. So they tired their horses and themselves, ran the fat off the steers and had no fun at all sitting around talking and getting to know one another.

Simple living has to be in touch with the physical environment. We walk in the real world, and the closer we can walk to what is not paved beneath us and not scraping the sky above us, we can simplify our lives. We learn to appreciate the free gifts of life—sunshine, snowflakes, change of seasons, the sounds of birds and the wonderful sound and feel of spring. We don't get in touch with our real world environment unless we can smell, feel and taste it as we walk in it.

My advice is to get out of your head. Get out of your books, perhaps even this one. Go out and start doing it. Do what you really want to do. Quit saying "I wish I could simplify." Don't fret and say, "I wish I didn't have so many things." Get rid of them. If you don't have enough imagination to locate the poor, to find people who could use your excess, then you must be called to something drastic like the bonfire I mentioned earlier. But when you do, don't confess the waste of material. Confess that you have no imagination, which is a much more serious offense. Perhaps some simplicity would help you with your imagination.

Conclusion: Worship

The Israelites worshipped a golden calf. We worship any gold. We've come a short way. In a culture that worships money, simple living is radically counter cultural. Theologically, it is refusing to worship the idol and insisting on the freedom to worship the one true God. If making and spending more and more money is the cultural way, then simple living is taking a powerful stand against it. Simple living stands in contradiction to the American way as it is usually understood because it does not subscribe to limitless accumulation.

Simple living calls us to reverence for all that is. We walk with gratitude and wonder. We do not allow ourselves to become dulled and insensitive to the beauty of the world. We learn to worship.

Our worshipful reverence then extends to people. We make space for a handshake, for eye contact. It is the complex and cluttered who create pretense and conventions that make our meetings superficial and dull.

"'Tis a gift to be simple, tis a gift to be free," as the Quakers sing. "'Tis a gift to come down where we ought to be." Simplicity requires our effort and I've detailed that effort, but it is also a gift, the grace of God. Our longing to be simple is often the sign of the presence of this grace. Simple living is a call to a path that is joyous and free because it is a type of love for God and those who need what you have, whether you know them or not. As Elizabeth Ann Seton, says, "Let us live simply so that others may simply live."

My quest now is to keep alert. To keep listening to how I feel about who I am and how others respond to that. I need to make sure I'm good news to myself, thereby being good news to others. My lifelong profession is to live the gospel. As Francis said, "Preach the gospel everywhere. Use words if necessary." It's who we are and the way we live that is the gospel message.

You will find your own good news through simple living because identity is not an idea, it is a lived reality. Simply do it. We all begin by making mistakes. The gospel says a lot about forgiving our mistakes. Perhaps we will always miscalculate, be too timid or overdo but we can always advance. One key is the absence of tension. Simple living calls us to creativity, but it is never a drain on energy, it is never stressful. We don't go around asking, "Am I living simply?" I find that if I'm questioning myself about it, I'm probably not. I believe that out of Jesus' gospel about sharing and doing without comes community with anyone who will be real. He prefers the company of those who were forced in one way or another to live simply. We choose to live simply. Evangelical or gospel poverty is a choice. I am entirely capable of earning and keeping much more money. I choose gospel poverty.

The gospel admonishes us not to hoard, not to fill our bellies and barns. That's misplaced faith. Instead we are to trust in the Lord. We don't put things under locks or entrust them to Prudential. They are not our security. The Lord is. The Lord says, "In faith you relate to me." The gospel message can be discovered in your own experience. The more you give, the more you get. The more you try to get rid of, the more things come back to you. The multiplication of loaves goes on in my life and will in yours. It goes on because I expect it to, because I know who is working the miracles. Sometimes it's about food, but it also has to do with gifts, inspirations and readiness to promote what is good in others.

Francis speaks of sweet Sister Simplicity. He speaks of her as sitting next to Wisdom. Poverty, even as a chosen way, is beneath simplicity. Poverty can get us groveling about and mixed up with all sorts of things. But there's a kind of clarity that comes with simplicity. We learn that when we make a choice, we create consequences. If we're not wise enough to foresee what will happen, experience will give us the data for making the next decision. I think this is at the heart of one of Francis' responses to one of the brothers. The brother came to Francis and said, "I am better educated than most of the brothers. I can read. We pray the office, but we share just a few books among us. I would love to have my own book to pray with. I could sit in solitude and contemplate the word. May I have my own office book for prayer?" Francis asked for three days to think it over.

After the three days he told the brother he would not be allowed to have his own office book. The surprised brother asked, "Why not?" Francis replied, "If you have your own office book, you will need a place to put it. If you have to have a place to put it, you will be searching for the proper place to put your office book, perhaps on a shelf or window ledge. Then, as long as that is where your office book is, it would make sense for you to have a chair near your book, so when you felt like praying, you could come and sit down at any time and pick up your book. But of course, if you have a chair in a certain place by your office book, other people will come by and say 'Oh, there's brother so-and-so's chair, don't sit in that. That's for him, because that goes with his office book, which goes with that ledge.' No. For you to have an office book is for you to have to start to plan how to acquire space, place, a chair, and privacy. So you will exclude the other brothers and you put yourself at a higher level. You may not have your own office book." It's clear when you are simple.

So, I know from experience that Simple Living promotes joy and freedom. I learned it most by laying St. Francis' attitude and teachings against the gospels. The teaching style of both Jesus and Francis was storytelling so I end this work with one more Franciscan story.

One day when Francis was walking in the woods, he was so filled with delight at the beauty of the world that he wished to express his gratitude with music. He had no violin, so he picked up two sticks and began to play. Birds sang and animals came out and danced. Far-fetched, you say? Perhaps only those who believe that animals dance can hear the violin music of two twigs.

Sweet Sister Simplicity lives on!